Original title:
The Attic of the Heart

Copyright © 2025 Creative Arts Management OÜ
All rights reserved.

Author: Matthew Whitaker
ISBN HARDBACK: 978-1-80587-166-8
ISBN PAPERBACK: 978-1-80587-636-6

Lanterns of Unseen Reflection

Dust bunnies dance in the light,
Old toys tell tales, oh what a sight!
Grandma's old hat, a quirky muse,
Whispers of laughter, a heart to use.

Frog-shaped lamps with missing eyes,
Chasing around like silly spies!
Memories flicker, even the weird,
In this odd space where dreams are sheered.

Captured Moments in Dim Retreats

Boxes stacked high, a treasure trove,
Old photos laugh, while the shadows rove.
Socks without pairs, a jumbled spree,
Ghosts of my youth, come dance with me!

A dusty old record spins tales of fun,
Dancing with nothing, oh, what a run!
Time held captive in hidden nooks,
Where echoes play like silly books.

Missed Connections and Faded Voices

A squeaky step on the wooden floor,
Echoes of nonsense from times of yore.
Letters kept safe, all crumpled and wry,
Sneaky old secrets that just won't die.

The clock strikes twelve with a hoot and a sigh,
Faded old hats, oh my, oh my!
Jumping through memories, a whimsical trip,
All in this space where lost friendships skip.

The Lanterns that Guided Us

Shadows stretch wide, with laughter they'll blend,
    Each trinket a story, each corner a friend.
    Mismatched mittens and a hat with a flair,
        In this funny maze, we float on air.

    The glow of old bulbs, a whimsical light,
    Illuminating joy through the giddy night.
    We stumble and giggle, in this cozy mess,
Finding sweet gems in our whimsical quest.

Keepsakes from the Past

Dusty socks and broken toys,
Memories lost in silly noise.
Nostalgia wrapped in a big old hat,
Worn by a cat who thinks it's fat.

Old cassette tapes and matching shoes,
Faded jeans with crazy hues.
Each box a treasure, a funny find,
All the quirks that shaped my mind.

Ghosts of Laughter and Tears

Echoes of giggles float in the air,
Chasing the cat, who just doesn't care.
A sock puppet dance in the middle of night,
Brought on by popcorn and flickering light.

Remember the time with the fizzy soda,
We sprayed the screen, what a wild quota!
Spirits of joy hang from the beams,
Teasing my heart with tickling dreams.

Portraits in Dim Light

Pictures of people with silly grins,
Trying to capture those lovable sins.
With goofy poses and awkward stances,
Their laughter still dances in quirky glances.

Each frame tells tales of a mismatched pair,
Like a dog in a bonnet, oh, if they dare!
Captured moments like time in a jar,
Remind me of who we really are.

Whispers Beneath the Slate Roof

Secrets of joy and playful schemes,
Whispers echo like childhood dreams.
Each rafter holds a story so sweet,
Of hide-and-seek behind little feet.

A tickle fight under blankets so warm,
Ghostly laughter that breaks every norm.
What treasures we hold in the shadows we keep,
Where giggles and whispers never sleep.

Tattered Pages of Yesterday

Dusty tomes filled with laughter,
Memories that twist and bend.
Witty tales of silly blunders,
With a punchline 'round the bend.

Cats in hats and dogs that dance,
Grandma's quirks on every page.
Spilling tea at every chance,
Oh, the joy of youthful rage.

Doodles drawn in margins wide,
Shopping lists turned into art.
Stories where the giggles hide,
Makes the mind and spirit start.

Flip through them with glee today,
Revisit each absurd delight.
In those pages, I'll always stay,
Laughing into the starry night.

Garlands of Old Regrets

Hanging hats from past mistakes,
Worn-out shoes from wild romance.
Dancing round a pot of flukes,
Making life a quirky dance.

A letter lost in translation,
Sent to someone far away.
Regrets made of strange elation,
In the backdrop of our play.

Old blue socks and mismatched gloves,
A heart that beats in funny ways.
Laughter gifts the life it loves,
Grinning through the silly days.

Each misstep is a patch of glee,
A garland 'round the neck of fate.
Embrace the chaos, wild and free,
Where joys and quirks regenerate.

The Lanterns We Never Lit

Flickering dreams in dusty jars,
Holding wishes never sung.
Lanterns left to collect dust,
Where hopes sit tight and young.

We planned a party for the stars,
With cupcakes dressed in silly hats.
But life got lost in crazy cars,
And now we're left with cats.

Old birthday candles, wishes blown,
Silly faces made with pies.
In this kitchen, laughter's grown,
While burnt toast still defies.

Yet every ember's brightened glow,
Reminds us of those whimsical nights.
So let's ignite, let laughter flow,
As we gather our fond delights.

Beneath the Roof of Remnants

Under eaves where echoes play,
Socks and shoes that never met.
Secrets that we hide away,
Like a pet that we forget.

Trinkets whisper tales of yore,
An alarm clock that won't chime.
Jokes shared as we hit the floor,
In a dance that laughs at time.

Chairs that creak with every tale,
Mayonnaise jars in silly stacks.
In shadows where our joys prevail,
Quirky relics make the cracks.

The roof may leak, the walls may bend,
But laughter lives where memories bloom.
In this world, we shall transcend,
Finding joy in every room.

The Dust of Lost Affection

In corners deep where memories hide,
Dust bunnies dance, take pride inside.
Forgotten vows wrapped in a shoe,
Wish me luck, I'm lost in stew.

Old love letters, crumpled and torn,
Waxed with feelings of the forlorn.
The cat sits smug on a worn-out chair,
While I search for what was once so rare.

There's a sock with holes, a runaway's tale,
Promises whispered, now frail and pale.
Laughter echoes from shadows cast,
As I chuckle at ghosts of a past.

In forgotten places, laughter still lingers,
With ghosts that tease and point their fingers.
I shuffle through memories caught off guard,
With a grin at the folly of my old heart card.

Songs of Memory in the Shadows

In the gloom where old tunes play,
Footloose memories dance and sway.
A broken record skips, then croons,
To echoes of long-forgotten tunes.

Beneath the beams of dusty light,
Nostalgia sings with all its might.
I trip on the notes, almost in glee,
As shadows chuckle at my off-key spree.

A concert of laughter, a clumsy beat,
With socks mismatched, I tap my feet.
Old photographs, with smiles so wide,
They wink at me, their joyful guide.

In this hall of fragments, joy is a tease,
As I dance with shadows, at my own ease.
What once felt heavy is light as air,
With songs of the past, I frolic and stare.

The Canvas of Melancholy Days

A canvas splattered with splotches bright,
Masterpieces made of mishap and fright.
Paint drips down, colors collide,
As I laugh at the chaos, not trying to hide.

Brush strokes whisper, tales of the woe,
Yet hidden in grief, the giggles still flow.
With each clumsy dab, a chuckle rings loud,
As I paint my confessions, both silly and proud.

Old paint tubes bursting, a messy affair,
Creating a portrait, almost too rare.
With each silly splash, I'm free to explore,
Memories echo like an off-key encore.

So here's to the canvas of days gone by,
Where sorrow and laughter so often comply.
In the gallery of life, I smile and display,
The vibrant confusion of a whimsical day.

Chests Full of Fleeting Glances

In corners where shadows play,
Dust bunnies dance, they sway.
Old love notes taped with care,
Whisper sweet nothings, if you dare.

Laughter echoes in each nook,
Forgotten toys, a storybook.
Clocks that clatter, time's disguise,
Painted dreams in old junk's eyes.

Mismatched socks give heartstrings tug,
An old cat sleeping, so snug.
Pickled memories in glass frames,
Even the paint still knows our names.

Among the junk, a treasure found,
A rubber chicken, silly sound.
Photos framed, smiles divine,
Oh, the joy of days gone by, so fine!

The Silence Between Heartbeats

In moments when silence sings,
A vacuum of forgotten things.
Leftover pizza on the shelf,
I ponder life and eat myself.

Coffee stains on ancient lore,
A garden gnome, I can't ignore.
The space between a tick and tock,
Where dreams unfurl like a funny sock.

Puppies bark and socks do hide,
Giggles float on the ceiling wide.
Every heartbeat hums a tune,
Underneath the laughing moon.

Whispers hide behind the door,
Echoes wearing socks, then more.
In stillness, where the giggles start,
A moment's joy unravels art.

Portraits of Time Unraveled

Old frames hang crooked on the wall,
Silly grins from the great hall.
Faded faces with wild hair,
Caught in moments, that we share.

Yesterday's fashion, what a sight,
Sequined jumpsuits, oh what a fright!
Time's portraits wear a comical crown,
Grinning wide, never a frown.

Cups of coffee stacked too high,
A jester's cap floats on by.
Balloons that never seem to pop,
Worn-out shoes that still won't stop.

Each brushstroke gives a wink,
In colors bright that never sink.
Captured laughter, life so bold,
In every picture, stories told.

Letters Never Sent

In stacks of paper, woes reside,
A quirky tale that missed the ride.
Ink blots mar a heartfelt aim,
Each scribbled thought, a funny name.

Sealed with tape, not a single stamp,
Ignored by time like an old lamp.
Words once bold now take a nap,
In an envelope hugging a gap.

Crumpled thoughts taste like the past,
While daydreams sprint, they go so fast.
Mismatched addresses, what a show,
Sent to places we'll never go.

Pigeons laugh as they fly away,
Wishing well in a goofy play.
In laughter, those letters still dwell,
Invisible echoes, they tell it well.

A Secret Sanctuary of Sentiment

In corners where old clothes hang,
Dust bunnies dance and old bells clang.
Mismatched socks in a loving heap,
Whispers of memories they gently keep.

Grandma's wig with a dusty charm,
Once a marvel, now a farm.
A treasure trove of silly hats,
Who knew that cats could wear such spats?

Beneath the beams, a giggle lurks,
Amid forgotten trinkets and jolly quirks.
A rubber chicken, a broken toy,
In a world of laughter, we find our joy.

So come and peek, but beware the trap,
For nostalgia's humor can give a slap.
Here laughter lives among the rust,
In this secret realm, joy's a must.

Windows to the Forgotten

Rusty panes that squeak and groan,
Peering through, we're not alone.
A pair of shoes with one lost lace,
Dreaming of adventures they used to chase.

A portrait of a cat, quite smug,
Sitting atop an old, furry rug.
Framed in dust, it seems to glare,
It holds the secrets of love and flair.

The chair that squeaks with every sigh,
Remembers laughter, or maybe a cry.
Each wobble tells a wily tale,
In this attic realm, we set our sail.

Hiding places, bright and dim,
A world of joy at the attic's brim.
From silly props to old parade,
In these windows, strange memories invade.

Timeless Echoes of Yesterday

Echoes float from dusty shelves,
A melody sung by forgotten elves.
Old board games missing a piece,
Claiming boredom's never a cease.

There's a clock that forgot to tick,
But still tells time, just not as quick.
It chuckles softly, 'Time's just a jest,
Relax, my friend, you need some rest.'

A pair of glasses with a whimsical glare,
Suggesting the future and past are a pair.
Old photos smile with faces so round,
In timeless frames, strange joy is found.

So tune your ears to the attic's song,
Where laughter dances and echoes belong.
With each creak, a laugh comes near,
Timeless tales told out of cheer.

Forgotten Love Letters in Dust

Letters curled with words of old,
Love notes hidden, stories untold.
In a box that's lost its way,
A romance bloomed, then went astray.

Each paper wrinkled, a tiny muse,
Scribbled hearts, oh what a ruse!
'Meet me by the big oak tree,'
Signed with a kiss, oh woe is me!

Some lines are sweet, some make you frown,
Like wearing a smile upside down.
A love that bloomed 'neath dusty beams,
Now tickles the heart with silly dreams.

So gather around and read with glee,
Forgotten words that dance on the sea.
In love's lost letters, laughter we'll find,
A treasure of joy, with memories intertwined.

Voices Carried by the Wind

Whispers dance upon the breeze,
Silly secrets in the trees.
Old socks argue with a shoe,
About a trip they never knew.

Laughter lingers in the air,
Chasing shadows everywhere.
Chairs complain of all the dust,
While the broom dreams of a gust.

A cat with wit climbs up the shelf,
Declaring proudly, 'I'm myself!'
The clock ticks jokes of days gone by,
While the moon winks an easy sigh.

Heartstrings Tied to Timeworn Spaces

In corners where the cobwebs play,
Dust motes dance the day away.
An old book sneezes from the shelf,
And laughs, 'I'm still alive myself!'

The rocking chair creaks a tune,
Of secrets shared beneath the moon.
A rubber band dreams of a fling,
While an old toy hums, 'I'm the king!'

Pictures grin from their frames tight,
Pretending they're the stars tonight.
A shoe with one lace stretched afar,
Claims it's training for a car.

Rhythms of a Dusty Melody

A piano plays a tune off-key,
Complaining, 'Where's the harmony?'
The dust bunnies drum on the floor,
Singing songs of days of yore.

Old chairs gossip with each squeak,
About the stories that they seek.
A grandma's hat, with plumes askew,
Winks and says, 'I still look new!'

Potatoes dream of being fries,
While curtains flutter with soft sighs.
The window laughs at passing clouds,
'You're not what you think, oh crowds!'

Latticed Horizons of Yesterday

Forgotten shoes line up to chat,
Discussing life beneath the mat.
A globe that spins, declaring bold,
'Travel is sweet but stories told!'

Math books chuckle of their scores,
While riddles hide behind closed doors.
A map unfolds with dreams astray,
In search of where the socks will play.

A grouchy chair tips back a bit,
Griping, 'I really need to sit!'
Yet here we dwell, with smiles wide,
In spaces where old dreams abide.

Treasures Beneath the Floorboards

Underneath the planks and beams,
A cat lies dreaming silly dreams.
Forgotten socks and balls so old,
And secrets still that won't be told.

A shoe from left but never right,
It must have taken quite a flight!
A treasure trove of junk we keep,
Made for laughter, not for sleep.

There's a sandwich from last month's feast,
A relic of a hungry beast.
With crumbs and laughter piled in heaps,
In the depths where memory sleeps.

So let's hold tight to what we find,
And cherish all that life designed.
For laughter lives among the dust,
In those odd places, that's a must!

Worn Pages of Longing

Old books stacked high up on the shelf,
With stories lost and tales of self.
They whisper softly, needing love,
As dust falls gently from above.

A romance hints at diy romance,
While recipes call for one last chance.
There are notes penned with crayon glee,
A heart in chaos, wild and free.

The pages turn with creaks and moans,
As laughter hides between the tones.
A temperately tragic plot,
Of heroes and cakes that burn a lot.

In margins thick, our scribbles dwell,
A mix of joy and all that fell.
For laughter swims in ink's embrace,
Through worn pages, time can't erase.

Cobwebbed Corners of Time

In corners dark where spiders scheme,
Old memories dance, a funny dream.
With webs so thick, they hold the past,
As if nostalgia's spells were cast.

A box of photos stacked askew,
With smiles and frowns from me to you.
Each laugh encased in shadowed light,
Twirling in the corners of night.

Here lies a hat with feathers bright,
Worn once to a comical fright.
A vintage coat adorned with pins,
That tells of fun and whimsical sins.

So swing by the edges, peek and see,
What laughter lives in history.
For in the dust, the joy's underlying,
In cobwebbed corners, always shining.

Fragments of What Once Was

In bits and pieces, joy can roam,
Old toys remind us of a home.
A doll with hair all frayed and bare,
And laughter stashed beyond the wear.

A broken kite, a jigsaw piece,
In those fragments, silly joy's increase.
Each memory swirls with playful grace,
A patchwork quilt of a happy place.

The game of hide and seek was grand,
When we once played, hand in hand.
But found me under piles of fluff,
With giggles echoing, never enough.

So cherish each odd little find,
In laughter's paths, we're intertwined.
For in fragments, whole hearts remain,
Crafting delight from joyful pain.

Footprints on the Wooden Floor

In corners where dust bunnies play,
Footprints dance in a funky ballet,
Old socks and shoes, a mismatched spree,
Whispers of laughter, just let them be.

A cat's meow mixes with a shoe's squeak,
Tales of mischief, oh so unique,
In this maze of memories and flair,
Who knew old wood would make us care?

A chair creaks softly in soft delight,
Echoes of parties that lasted till night,
Each plank a story, each crack a song,
Yet with every thud, the blame's never wrong.

So tiptoe lightly, don't wake the past,
In this quirky space, the moments last,
For laughter lingers as shadows sway,
On this wooden floor where dreams come to play.

Nestled Tales Behind Closed Doors

Secrets hide where we dare not peek,
In drawers stuffed with odd, antique geek,
Old toys and books, a comical scene,
Where gnomes might rove and bumblebees lean.

Jars filled with buttons, a colorful crew,
Spilling tales of a once merry brew,
Each clink and clatter, a giggle inside,
Behind every door, a whimsical ride.

A coat hangs awkwardly, with stories to tell,
Of dance-offs and mishaps at the local swell,
While wobbly shelves hold a trophy from youth,
A reminder of shenanigans after the truth.

So venture in, and let laughter ignite,
Those nestled tales reach great heights of delight,
For behind those doors, joy persists and roars,
Unfolding the laughter in forgotten shores.

Dreams Beneath the Shingles

A pile of dreams stacked high like old bricks,
With stories of clowns and some odd slick tricks,
Under shingles where echoes collide,
A funhouse mirror for all to confide.

The craziest hats and mismatched shoes,
Whisk away worries, erase the blues,
Beneath surreal skies of forgotten bliss,
Where mischief and mayhem gleefully kiss.

Puppets of yarn wave hello with a grin,
Crafting a world where giggles begin,
As raindrops tap-dance a rhythm so spry,
Beneath these shingles, our hopes can fly high.

So bring your quirks, let your heart roam,
In this attic of whimsy, we'll find a home,
Where dreams are not heavy, but light as a feather,
And laughter's our glue, now and forever.

The Grains of Time Forgotten

In a timeworn clock with tick-tock flair,
Grains of laughter float on the air,
Moments slip by like sand in a bowl,
Each tick a reminder, we're all on a roll.

Old looms spin threads of jest and delight,
As time does a dance in the soft golden light,
With comical tales of the days gone past,
Reminding us sweetness is never too fast.

Weaving through hours with twists in the seams,
Chasing old shadows that carry our dreams,
So scoop up the giggles, let memories unfold,
In the grains of time, a treasure of gold.

With each passing hour, we craft our own fate,
Embrace every chuckle and celebrate,
For in the laughter lies wisdom untold,
In the grains of time, our smiles will hold.

Requiem for the Long-Lost

In the depths of a dusty space,
Old socks and toys begin to race.
Dust bunnies dance with a squeaky sound,
Lost treasures waiting, just hanging around.

Forgotten jeans, a shirt with a tear,
Whispering secrets in the stale air.
A sandwich wrapped, aged like a vow,
What a feast they must have in their retro show!

Mice with a mission, pitter-pat feet,
Hosting a party, oh what a treat!
While memories flit like moths in the light,
They giggle and brag about lost disco nights.

So raise a glass to the stuff we discard,
A toast to the clutter, it's never too hard.
For inside these walls, laughter gleams bright,
In the echoes of things that vanished from sight.

Sighs Between Forgotten Pages

In books that are stacked and piled so high,
The covers are wrinkled, time to say goodbye.
Whispers of stories cling to the spine,
Where plots meet the dust and secrets entwine.

A recipe lost for a cake gone stale,
Instructions include a curious tale.
Baking mishaps with egg on my face,
My kitchen's a comedy, a culinary chase!

Old letters cackling, 'What were we thinking?'
As inked villains laugh while our lives keep shrinking.
They flirt with the dust, a scandalous cheer,
"I loved you once," they echo, drawing near.

So breathe in the scent, that sweet musty air,
With sagas of love and great daring flair.
For every page turned, a giggle remains,
In the sighs between stories, where laughter reigns.

The Stillness of Breathing Memories

In corners where silence takes a quick nap,
Whimsical whispers emerge from the trap.
Maps of our childhood, forgotten and worn,
Plotting adventures where laughter is born.

A clock on the wall, with its tick tock delight,
Races memories past like a kite in flight.
Each pause a chuckle, each second a jest,
Life's funny punchlines we can't help but quest.

Peeking through shadows, a ghostly parade,
Friends from the past don't seem to have stayed.
Snickers of tales, absurd and sublime,
Tickling our hearts with their mischievous rhyme.

So let's gather 'round with a grin and a sigh,
For memories linger, they never say die.
In the stillness of laughter, our stories will glow,
With joy we remember what we used to know.

Curtains Drawn Against Time

Behind closed curtains, secrets loom free,
Chasing the sunlight, they giggle with glee.
Old shoes hold tales of a dance long ago,
The rhythm still echoes, a delightful show.

With each passing day, the mirror politely,
Reflects all our mishaps, smiling so rightly.
The hairdos of yesteryears laugh in surprise,
While outfits proclaim, "Who wore this disguise?"

Pineapple pictures and silly old hats,
Grinning in frames, recalling the spats.
Laughter like bubble wrap pops in the air,
As curtains come down, no moment to spare.

So here's to the chaos, the fun and the clatter,
To moments we treasure, let's raise a good chatter.
In corners and folds where giggles unwind,
With curtains drawn tightly, our joys are enshrined.

The Partition of Crumpled Wishes

In corners dark, the dreams do hide,
With socks and mittens, side by side.
A paper airplane, aging fast,
It's flown so high, yet fell at last.

Doodles smile on crumpled sheets,
As absent-minded kids' heartbeats.
The cereal box, a treasure chest,
Where mom's old recipes still rest.

Forgotten toys from years ago,
They play a game, called 'Who Wants to Show?'
In shadows thick, they plot a scheme,
To bring back laughter, spark a dream.

Yet memories twist like silly straws,
In laughter's grip, we hail applause.
With each odd find, a chuckle flies,
In crumpled wishes, joy complies.

In Between the Gaps of Memory

Where laughter hangs in dusty air,
A fallen beard from Christmas fair.
Tickling tales from grandpa's chair,
Mixed with the smell of mom's despair.

A birthday cake, just crumbs remain,
Mismatched candles, a comical gain.
We laugh at faces made in haste,
As icing spills, no cake to waste!

In corners dim, a photo's glare,
Of outfits strange that none would wear.
Our childhood selves in foolish poses,
A garden full of blooming roses.

So sip the tea with quilted pride,
And share the tales we can't abide.
For in the gaps, the giggles twine,
In jumbled minds, our hearts align.

Stained Glass of Past Emotions

A shattered heart in colors bold,
With every hue, a tale retold.
Through laughter's prisms, tears roll bright,
In rainbow shades, missing the light.

The jokes we cracked at all the wrong times,
A symphony of silly rhymes.
With rusted toys and candy wraps,
Old feelings play in malleable traps.

In windows framed by yesterday,
Old gags and quirks are on display.
As memories dance like circus clowns,
Their painted smiles erase our frowns.

So raise a glass to colored woes,
For laughter finds where memory goes.
With every piece, the joy's amassed,
In stained glass, our love's steadfast.

Lanterns in the Misdirection

In fumbled darkness, candles flicker,
Guiding the lost and the snicker.
A misplaced sock, a funny hat,
These lanterns glow, revealing splat!

With wrong turn signs that lead us here,
We drift through nights, fueled by cheer.
The wayward glow of puns so bright,
Filling the gaps with reckless light.

Objects dance in the glimmer's sway,
A jester's cap from yesterday.
As giggles chase the dust away,
Misdirection leads to laughter's play.

So let them shine, those lamps of jest,
In every heart, they play their best.
For when we're lost, we'll find a way,
With lanterns bold, we'll laugh and stay.

Threads of Love Woven Tight

In the corner sits an old stuffed cat,
With one ear missing, he looks quite fat.
He tells me stories, oh so absurd,
Of socks that vanished without a word.

Dust bunnies dance with forgotten toys,
Their laughter echoes, oh what noise!
Secrets and giggles wrapped in delight,
Who knew lost things could be such a sight?

A chair that squeaks like a ghostly crew,
It creaks out jokes that aren't quite true.
I laugh so hard, I almost cry,
What a strange place where memories lie!

Oh, the labels on jars, quite an array,
That once held snacks from a happier day.
Each sticky note tells of love and plight,
In this cozy nook, everything feels right.

The Ghosts of What Was

There's a sock that just refuses to pair,
A lone wanderer without a care.
Ghosts of laundry past, they come to tease,
Living in chaos, oh what a breeze!

A tea set gathering lovely dust,
Its porcelain smiles, so gentle and rust.
They reminisce of parties not begun,
With laughter bubbling just for fun.

Old photos yell of hair that's gone wild,
Each snapshot holds an unruly child.
With goofy grins and silly poses,
This attic's charm forever composes.

The ghosts prance lightly, they know the drill,
Turning the past into whimsical thrill.
Oh, the mischief in the shadows cast,
In this quirky space, I'm free at last!

Sifting Through the Layers of Us

A box of crayons, terribly bent,
Each color fades but the memories scent.
Drawings of dreams on the walls so bright,
Sifting through layers, what a delight!

Forgotten hats in a whimsical stack,
One's too big, and another's black.
I wear them all, a clownish display,
Laughing at life in a joyous way!

Once there was a diary, locked up tight,
With love notes hidden by giggles of fright.
Its pages whisper secrets in the night,
Sifting through laughter, everything feels right.

Old board games waiting to be played,
Where champions rise and memories fade.
We roll the dice, our bonds intertwine,
In this layered love, everything's fine!

Hidden Nooks of Nostalgia

Behind the door, a blanket fort waits,
Where dreams collide and laughter creates.
With stuffed bears guarding our silly quests,
In hidden nooks, we find our best rests.

A mismatched teacup, chipped but sweet,
Holds stories and giggles—such a treat!
We sip imaginary tea, oh what fun,
In this alcove of joy, we're forever young.

Crumbs of cookies from a time long past,
Remind us of baking our first batch, fast.
Who knew that flour could fly so high?
In these hidden spots, we never say bye.

A thimble collection, each with a tale,
Of stitches and seams and the wind in the sail.
With each little treasure, a wink and a nod,
In the nooks of nostalgia, life feels so broad.

Shattered Reflections of Togetherness

Mirrors crack with laughter's plot,
Friends gather, sharing silly thoughts.
Dusty jokes beneath the eaves,
Tickling memories, no one leaves.

Coffee spills on forgotten dreams,
Laughter bursts at the seams.
Old photos wink with a grin,
Past shenanigans, we reel them in.

Underneath the cluttered pile,
Old toys dance, staying awhile.
Socks with holes tell tales of shame,
Yet in this chaos, we're the same.

Each tale told is tattered yet bright,
In togetherness, we own our plight.
In laughter's arms, we gladly sway,
Turning mishaps into play.

The Chamber of Unfulfilled Dreams

Dusty boxes hide schemes gone wild,
Plans for fame from a hopeful child.
Yet here they sit, with cobwebs dressed,
Improvised roles in an ongoing jest.

Ambitions sing their fractured tune,
Broken promises, a lopsided moon.
Outdated gadgets, lost in time,
Collecting dust, but still in rhyme.

Riddles lost in a playful haze,
Fancies forgotten in a daze.
We chase the stars without a care,
Knocking over dreams here and there.

Yet amidst clutter, joy persists,
Finding humor is on our list.
In every shattered hope we find,
A chuckle waiting—oh so kind!

Echoes of Heartfelt Whispers

Whispers flutter like moths in queues,
Tales of crushes and old blues.
Laughter rolled with every sigh,
Each secret shared, a pie in the sky.

Pretend romance in the attic's air,
Couples giggling with nary a care.
Sticky notes of love declared,
Pranks and confessions, slightly impaired.

Old records play timeless tunes,
Dance parties with brooms as loons.
Echoed giggles in the night,
Summer's flame, a delight so bright.

Casting shadows of memory's delight,
Each giggle a spark, joy takes flight.
In the silence, our hearts still cheer,
In whispered secrets, laughter's near.

Crumbling Dreams on Sheltered Beams

Old beams creak with forgotten schemes,
Hopes piled high like silly dreams.
Cat-like antics, joys once bold,
Each slip a story, jovially told.

Lopsided shelves hold curious things,
Nostalgic tunes that memory sings.
Sock puppets grinning, two in a row,
Performing antics, putting on a show.

Amidst crumbling thoughts, we find our way,
Building castles in disarray.
Mismatched socks in a playful dance,
Life's odd treasures give joy a chance.

With laughter echoing, dreams fade slow,
In our folly, love's laughter grows.
In this funny realm, we remain,
Finding joy in every grain.

The Path to Forgotten Sorrows

In corners where the shadows creep,
Old giggles echo from the heap.
Lost socks hold secrets, a mysteries weave,
While teacups whisper; who'd believe?

A prized collection of dust and cheer,
Worn-out memories float near.
Footsteps skip through piles of old,
Recounting stories silly and bold.

Giggles bounce off the peeling walls,
As shadows dance at the whim of calls.
Each item a treasure, a tiny jest,
Imbued with laughter, they jest the best.

So here in the nooks where the sunlight bends,
We'll find the laughter that never ends.
With every glance back, a chuckle shines,
In this clutter, joy intertwines.

Dustbunnies and Dreams Deferred

Fluffy dustbunnies make grand escapes,
Drafty coattails of old winter capes.
They conspire and plot their next great stunt,
While the mothball army plans a fun hunt.

Old dreams stacked high like boxes of cheese,
Whispering hopes with a gentle breeze.
Who knew that wishes could gather such grime?
They're waiting for a jolt, just give them some time.

What treasures did we leave buried below?
Nostalgic giggles, when will they show?
Under layers of 'just maybe' and 'not yet',
Lay the remnants of joy we won't forget.

So we dust off the laughter, release all the woes,
On a carpet of yarn where the silliness grows.
For memories linger like moths in the light,
With dreams in our pockets, we'll take off in flight.

Glimpses of Abandoned Hopes

Peeking past curtains of faded despair,
A glimpse of a toy soldier, brave in his wear.
Every misplaced shoe holds an adventure rare,
With dreams of grand battles fought in the air.

Dusty old jars filled with odd bits and ends,
Giggles rise where the whimsy transcends.
Forgotten ambitions dance like a breeze,
In the laughter of echoes, we find our ease.

Chasing reflections that spark in the gloom,
The hope of tomorrow can brighten this room.
Each trinket and token, a project on pause,
Reviving ambitions with comedic applause.

So lift up your spirits, let worries depart,
While we rummage through visions stitched into art.
For even in sorrow, a grin can be found,
In the tapestry woven where joy is unbound.

Reflections on Wooden Beams

The beams overhead hold wisdom so vast,
Reporting tales of a turbulent past.
Yet they whisper softly with each creak and sigh,
Rewarding the dreamers, oh my, oh my!

In the nooks of the rafter, a wild cat naps,
While dust motes swirl like whimsical maps.
They show us the pathways of what once has been,
As the heart of the house gives a cheeky grin.

Funny how laughter can light up a space,
A wink from the woodwork, an old friendly face.
With every reflection, a spark reignites,
In the hall of mischief, where nonsense delights.

So let's raise a glass to this old, cozy haunt,
Where memories linger, and follies can flaunt.
In the shadows of beams, we'll dance and we'll hum,
For laughter is timeless—even when it's from scum!

Memories Wrapped in Silk

In a corner, old sweaters hide,
Each with tales of laughs and pride.
A squeaky toy, long lost to time,
Whispers jokes like a nursery rhyme.

Dust bunnies dance on the wooden floor,
While moths debate what they're looking for.
A photo of me with hair gone wild,
Caught in a moment, laughter compiled.

A teacup with a chip sings a song,
Of tea parties where I thought I belonged.
The cat's in the hat, pretending to read,
Sipping my dreams like it's all I need.

These silly trinkets, so much to see,
Hold memories wrapped up in glee.
Like a time machine that loves to play,
Each find brings a smile to my day.

Inside the Heart's Cloister

Behind those doors, a treasure trove,
Where mismatched socks and giggles rove.
A rubber chicken, bright and spry,
Still cracks me up; oh my, oh my!

Forgotten books with dusty spines,
Share silly tales and comical lines.
In an old shoe, an adventure rests,
Waiting for a friend's bold quests.

Jokes scribbled on napkins from last year,
Remind me of the friendships dear.
A tin of cookies, empty and worn,
Crumbs of laughter, tales reborn.

In this quiet nook, joy reigns supreme,
A playful corner, a daydream.
With every peek, there's magic aglow,
Inside this cloister, let laughter flow.

Silenced Songs of a Bygone Era

Old records spin with ghostly cheer,
Each crackle has a story to hear.
With dance parties held for just one,
I'm both the star and the audience, fun!

A broken guitar, strummed once at noon,
Now sings soft tunes with a sleepy croon.
The sock puppet waits, eager to play,
Whispers punchlines from yesterday.

Jokes carved on shelves, bold as can be,
Brought back the giggles that once were free.
The old clock winks, slightly askew,
Laughing at time that just flew.

In this room, a comedy show,
With echoes of laughter in every toe.
Silenced songs now tickle the ear,
Buried deep, they reappear.

Dusty Delights of the Soul

A wobbly chair tells tales of old,
Where wild imaginations boldly unfold.
Dusty delights, like a pie gone wrong,
Serve up a slice of a joyful song.

Old games lie waiting, all out of tune,
To resurrect smiles beneath the moon.
With mismatched shoes, we dance through the grime,
Every misstep just adds to the rhyme.

The lamp flickers, sharing a wink,
As I dig deeper than I dare think.
With a flip of a toy, the room comes alive,
A jester's harlequin, ready to thrive.

From lively banter to echoes of cheer,
These dusty delights bring memories near.
In every shadow, a chuckle is spun,
A wink from the past, reminding it's fun.

Intricate Footnotes of Afternoons Past

Socks mismatched, with a grin so wide,
The cat on a quest, with nothing to hide.
Sticky fingers from candy delight,
Chasing the dog, what a hilarious sight.

Under the table, whispers abound,
Last week's secrets, now lost, never found.
A treasure map drawn in crayon so bright,
Leading to treasures in the middle of the night.

Grandpa's old stories, a laugh and a sigh,
He swears he once flew with a pie in the sky.
The couch is a fort, with blankets, it's true,
Where dragons live on the other side of the blue.

Ice cream for dinner, why not, who will tell?
With giggles and chaos, we weave our own spell.
Cherished footnotes of laughter and glee,
Each afternoon spills wild, just you wait and see.

Hushed Lullabies of Summer Nights

Fireflies dance in a twilight parade,
The neighbors build castles, so unafraid.
With crickets as conductors on soft lullaby,
We sing off-key under a starry sky.

Sneaking a snack, marshmallows galore,
On top of a s'more, so much to explore.
The dog joins the chorus with a silly bark,
While shadows grow tall in the fading dark.

Mom says it's bedtime, but we whisper and plot,
Dreams filled with giggles and all that we're not.
A circus of laughter, what chaos we weave,
Each summer night's tale, we boldly believe.

The moon winks at us, with a gentle glow,
As we drift off to lands where the wild things roam.
With hushed, silly lullabies crooning on high,
Let's be brave adventurers until morning's sigh.

Unraveling in the Twilight's Embrace

Oh, the mischief that stirs when the daylight fades,
In shorts and mismatched shoes, the fun never evades.
Ghost stories giggled, all nonsense and flair,
We conjure up monsters made of soft teddy bear.

The shadows twist games, like old friends we greet,
Hide and seek chaos in the cool evening heat.
A pie made of dirt, served with a grin,
"Delicious!" we cheer, as we dig right in!

Whispers of pranksters, don't wake up the bear,
A pillow fort built like an old millionaire.
To sail on a ship made of cushions and dreams,
With pirates and treasures, or so it seems.

Crickets join our laughter, as we weave our tale,
Until yawns take hold, and we set our sails.
Unraveling softly in twilight's warm grace,
Finding hilarity in every sweet embrace.

Footfalls Through the Quieter Halls

Sneaky little footfalls, tiptoeing near,
Whispers of secrets we hold so dear.
The clock chimes local gossip on the wall,
It knows all the stories, quite proud of it all.

A napping cat sprawls, embracing its dreams,
While we raid the pantry, laughing it seems.
The ancient vacuum, a monster so sly,
Makes us all jump when it lets out a cry.

In the quietest corners, treasures are found,
A cookie crumb trail leads us around.
We dodge grandpa's slippers - a quick daring game,
As laughter erupts, it's us that's to blame.

Old portraits look down, with eyes of surprise,
At our antics unfolding before their wise eyes.
Through the quieter halls, we're kings of the night,
With footfalls like thunder, our spirits take flight.

Chasing Echoes of What Once Was

In a groan of wood and dust,
Memories play their tricks,
A sock from twenty years ago,
And a cat that chases sticks.

The laughter settles like old wine,
Fizzing up in forgotten jars,
We'd jump if we heard someone call,
But it's just our old guitars.

The playground just outside my mind,
Swings that squeak like old folks' knees,
We run, we leap, we try to fly,
But land in piles of autumn leaves.

With echoes of youth ringing clear,
We dance in circles of lost cheer,
Each twirl's a laugh, each shout a shout,
Chasing what we can't live without.

The Dreams We Left Behind

A pile of dreams in a corner,
Most are silly, but quite divine,
One's a rocket, another's a cat,
Oh, how they all intertwine!

Ghosts of plans that went astray,
Float around like cotton candy,
A bakery list from '95,
Only made the crumbs quite dandy.

The pajamas worn for too many nights,
Sit like relics of sorts,
Worn thin and faded with the years,
Perfect for awkward retorts.

Yet in that dreamland of might-have-beens,
Wanderlust yells "Let's take a stroll!"
We run barefoot through puddles of thought,
Waving our silly, wild souls.

Cider and Stars Under the Roof

Bubbles of cider dance on tongues,
While tales bounce off the painted walls,
Silly stories, contagious grins,
Under the roof where laughter calls.

Fireflies mix with autumn cheer,
An old hat perched, like a crown,
We toast to nights that felt too short,
As silly fables tumble down.

Of wishes made to unwind time,
And stars that twinkle with delight,
We sip and smile at mischief done,
As moonbeams guide our wild flight.

Each chuckle wraps us like a quilt,
In dreams that dance like floating leaves,
A banquet of joy, unfold and spill,
Cider and stars, our hearts reprieve.

Under Layers of Silence and Light

Whispers play like tag in the air,
Tracing patterns no one can see,
A lightbulb flickers with every thought,
A spark of laughter, wild and free.

Under the layers where dust bunnies dwell,
Ideas roll like forgotten balls,
They bounce and giggle at the past,
In corners where quietness calls.

A chair creaks with tales untold,
It holds secrets of who we were,
In the kaleidoscope of memories,
Life spins, twirls, and makes us blur.

So come and lift the veils, my friend,
Let's paint the silence with vivid hues,
For beneath the stillness and dim-lit joy,
Lies a canvas brimming with views.

Nostalgia's Silent Chamber

In the corner sits a shoe,
That once danced on a table for two.
Its partner is lost, oh what a shame,
But it still sits proud, playing the game.

Old photos hang like portraits of fright,
Of hairdos that scream, 'What was that night?'
We all struck a pose, yes, quite the sight,
Now we laugh at our past, oh what a delight!

A grandpa clock ticks, but its hands are stalled,
Time's taken a break, or maybe just mauled.
It tells stories of when we forgot to be wise,
Now we're dodging memories in a comic disguise.

Dust bunnies dance like they own the place,
In polka-dot skirts, with a nonchalant grace.
They wink at old secrets and giggle at fate,
While I sip my tea and just contemplate.

Treasures of the Soul's Vault

A hat with a feather, bright and absurd,
Worn by a youth who was quite the wordbird.
It quells the old thoughts of disco and flare,
Yet fits like a crown that's way too rare.

A music box plays the tune of some woe,
But its melody's stuck in the year '82,
When all we knew were the steps to the beat,
And the only concern was matching our feet.

Books piled high, with dust and with glee,
Filled with the truths of who we used to be.
They whisper of summers with no cares around,
Each page an adventure, where joy could be found.

A rubber chicken: the relic that sings,
Reminding us all of the silly old things.
It squeaks out a laugh when times get too tough,
Proving that laughter is always enough.

Cobwebs of Old Affections

In each nook lies a memory sweet,
Wrapped up in cobwebs, a delicate treat.
They tickle the nose with a whisper of cheer,
While I smile through dust at the love I hold dear.

Old valentines flutter like moths in the dark,
With scribbles of hearts and an awkward remark.
Some promise the moon, some promise the sun,
Yet here on the shelf, they all seem like fun.

A soft teddy bear, with one eye gone shy,
It once had a voice, oh my, oh my!
Now it just sits, with a grin and a wink,
A guardian of secrets we never might think.

A broken clock, forever stuck at twelve,
Holds the moment when we first found ourselves.
Yet here it still lays, both silly and wise,
Time's just a game, to play with our sighs.

Chests of Lost Yearnings

A chest full of wishes, with dreams on the side,
Each one a voyage, a wild, funny ride.
Some are ballooned, others feel flat,
Yet I open them up and laugh at the chat.

Mismatched socks, they tell tales of their own,
Of dances in kitchens, of laughter that's grown.
Now they lie waiting, like treasures untold,
Whispering secrets of friendships so bold.

A boombox rests like a king on its throne,
With mixtapes of passion, laughter, and tone.
It's waiting for someone to press play once more,
And relive those moments of an impromptu floor.

The echoes of jokes still linger around,
Each punchline a stamp on the years that we've browned.

We laugh with a wink, drink tea from a cup,
In this space we find joy: forever enough.

Memories Wrapped in Cobwebs

In the corner, dusty dreams hide,
Where the old teddy bears still abide.
A pirate's treasure, a rubber duck,
And candy wrappers—all gone amok.

Forgotten trinkets, a timeworn sock,
Crammed in a box—what a funny stock!
Ghosts of laughter in the air,
Tickle my nose, but I don't care!

Each cobweb spins stories of yore,
Like socks that vanished—who knows the score?
A floppy hat with oversized flair,
Whispers of mischief hang everywhere.

So, let the laughter unfold and play,
As I sift through memories of yesterday.
With every giggle that dust may part,
I find a piece of my silly heart.

Echoes of Childhood Laughter

Giggles echo in the hall,
As I stumble through it all.
A secret hideout behind the stairs,
Where imaginary friends have wild affairs.

Crayon monsters on the walls dance,
Remind me of a candy-flavored trance.
Squeaky shoes on an old wood floor,
Growing up was never a bore!

The goldfish bowl, a throne of dreams,
Where I crowned my knight with ketchup streams.
Each pop of bubblegum, a new delight,
Turning a rainy day so bright.

Oh, the echoes swirl and twirl,
In this charming little world.
With every chuckle from the past me,
I chuckle too, oh what a spree!

Shadows of Unspoken Words

In the shadows of a quiet night,
Like whispers hidden from the light.
A secret joke, a chuckle retained,
In the silence, laughter's remained.

Balloons that drifted too high to catch,
And games we played with strings to attach.
With every glance, a story untold,
Where surprises shimmer in colors bold.

The shadows tease with playful glee,
Eye rolls and snickers, oh, can it be?
With every smile cloaked in jest,
Unspoken words surely are best.

So let the night unearth the mirth,
As I tumble through my nostalgic worth.
For every shadow has a punchline bright,
That glows and giggles in the night.

Treasures in the Gloom

Amongst the clutter, my heart does roam,
Through tangled yarn and mismatched combs.
A rubber chicken and a hat with flair,
These treasures bloom in the dark, laid bare.

Old love letters with doodles and hearts,
Bring back the smiles; they're works of arts.
In the gloom, I find unexpected cheer,
Like glittery socks that once disappeared!

Forgotten photos, goofy grins,
Remind me that where humor begins.
Tickles and tumbles that warm the soul,
Make the dust bunnies feel less like a toll.

So here's to the treasures, odd and spry,
That make me laugh until I cry!
In the shadows, I'll always find,
Gems of joy, lovingly entwined.

Skies Behind the Eaves

Up in the rafters, where the dust bunnies play,
Jokes hang like cobwebs, all tangled in gray.
Laughter drips down like rain on the floor,
Echoes of giggles, who could ask for more?

Old shoes rest on beams, with a tale to tell,
Of shoehorn struggles and slipping quite well.
The cat weaves through shadows, a phantom of grace,
Chasing dreams hidden in a forgotten space.

A squeezy old chair where the memories sit,
Creaks like a chorus, but never admits.
Socks lost to the ages, playing hide and seek,
To find them again, you just might need a peek!

Living up high, where the giggles reside,
Every squeak and rattle, our silly guide.
A treasure of joy in this whimsical sphere,
There's no better attic, our laughter's sincere!

Reverie Among the Raftered Stars

Stars dance on beams that creak and sigh,
Wishing we knew what's up there in the sky.
The moon winks at us, all comfy and bright,
While we crack open stories, giggles take flight.

Dust motes swirl round like tiny ballerinas,
Twisting and twirling in daydreamy kitchens.
A blanket of starlight, a sprinkle of cheer,
Whispers of laughter are all that you hear.

The chimney's a dragon, with smoke as its plume,
Breathing out stories that fill up the room.
With each little chuckle, a constellation grows,
A galaxy formed where the silliness flows.

Here's a place where the serious do fade,
And every routine just feels like a charade.
In this topsy-turvy, our humor will rise,
Building dreams in the rafters, beneath moonlit skies!

Shadows of Unspoken Words

Whispers of secrets float high on the beams,
Each one an echo from playful daydreams.
A shadow of folly drapes light on the wall,
As laughter spills out, there's room for us all.

A singed old paper from a prank gone astray,
Tell tales of mischief in the light of the day.
Rabbits and robots play hopscotch in air,
In corners forgotten, the joy becomes rare.

A thump from below, did the ghost trip again?
We giggle together, what a fun little sin!
Unspoken words dance like dust in the light,
Creating a hush in the midst of our night.

But here in this space, where silliness thrives,
We treasure the chaos and all of our lives.
Through shadows we laugh, with a soft, gentle mirth,
A sweet serenade from the corners of worth.

Hidden Corners of Emotion

In the nooks and the crannies, where giggles abide,
We stash all our glee and some feelings inside.
Crayons are scribbled on papers all torn,
Doodles of joy, in the nightlight are born.

A rubber band ball, it's a colorful mess,
Much like our hearts, at times in distress.
Banana peels slide by, a slapstick surprise,
In corners we find where our silliness lies.

A pop of confetti, it bursts through the gloom,
Each shimmer reflects all our hopes in the room.
Tickling the edges of feelings too real,
While laughter entwines with the sorrow we feel.

From the hidden corners, we conjure a smile,
Life's quirks wrapped in joy, let's laugh for a while.
In every small nook, our emotions can spark,
Creating a symphony as bright as the lark!

Cracks in the Ceiling of Memory.

Up in the rafters, laughter spills,
Forgotten jokes that give us chills.
A dusty joke book, well out of date,
Tells tales of love from a strange first date.

Old toys lie wasted, covered in fluff,
A rubber duck that's had way enough.
His quack now sounds like an awkward gaff,
Yet, every glance makes me break into a laugh.

Amidst cobwebs where no one peeks,
Lies a sock puppet that still speaks.
He tells lost stories when humor is slack,
And if you giggle, he'll hurl them back.

Memories bubble like soda gone flat,
Twinges of joy where I once sat.
In this space of highs and lows,
I occasionally trip on forgotten toes.

Whispers of Forgotten Dreams

In the corner sits a tattered dream,
Muffled laughter, a silent scream.
An old snore echoing 'til dawn,
Tracing paths that were once drawn.

A chicken in a tutu does a dance,
Did I ever think this was my chance?
Balloons float high, but one's gone rogue,
I'm left grappling with a memory fog.

On the shelf, an LP spins alone,
With every scratch, I hear a groan.
Songs of yore in a garbled croon,
Karaoke night would've made me swoon!

These whispers tickle the corners of night,
And bring to life my misfit plight.
With a chuckle, I pull back the veil,
Knowing dreams don't always set sail.

Dusty Chests of Longing

Under the stairs lies a chest of lore,
Filled with treasures I can't ignore.
A broken clock that ticks far too slow,
Once held time like a strange burlesque show.

Old letters wrinkled, yellowed with age,
Some scribbles read like a scripted page.
An ex once wrote quite a silly rhyme,
Rhymes about our favorite crime!

Scattered trinkets and mismatched socks,
Among the chaos, a curious box.
Inside, a slinky is quietly curled,
Tangled up in my whimsical world.

With every rustle, a giggle escapes,
At the memories and silly shapes.
These dusty chests hold laughter entrapped,
In the longing of times I happily napped.

Secrets Beneath the Eaves

Beneath the eaves, where shadows play,
Lies a secret stash of yesterday.
An umbrella that once ruled the rain,
Now pops open in a moment of pain.

Paintings lean with a crooked smile,
Each askew canvas tells a tale worthwhile.
Monsters balance on the edge of dreams,
While giggles intermingle with moonbeams.

A cupboard squeaks with a knowing grin,
Stored within are pasts thick and thin.
Every surprise that pops out with flair,
Leaves me rolling in nostalgic air.

In this attic of whimsy and cheer,
Laughter lingers, it's ever near.
Secrets dance in the twilight glow,
Witty moments steal the show.

Whispers of Forgotten Love

In a corner, a shoe with a tale,
Its partner's long gone; it's doomed to fail.
Love letters crumbled, their ink now a blur,
Like old socks that think they still once were.

A bouquet of dust sits still on the floor,
Once bright pink roses now ashes and more.
They whisper sweet things you can't quite recall,
Like the joke about love that sparked quite a fall.

A mirror reflects the hair of a cat,
That once had a crush on the neighbor's fat rat.
The laughter still lingers, a tickle, a tease,
As they danced on the rooftops, swaying with ease.

So let's open the box of silly old dreams,
Where laughter and love burst at all the seams.
Among crumpled visions and notes thrown away,
A clown car of memories is here to stay.

Dusty Dreams and Secrets

In the shadow of boxes, a teddy bear grins,
With secrets of ages, and dust on its chin.
Giggles echo softly from centuries past,
As the riddles of youth entertain and amass.

Beneath an old blanket, a rabbit peeks through,
With tales of adventures no one ever knew.
He chuckles at dreams that once made him scream,
Like the time that the cat stole his plush carrot dream.

An old photograph shows a dance on a chair,
With mismatched socks and way too much hair.
Each snapshot remembers the joy and the mess,
While winking at life in its fluffy red dress.

So here in this place where the laughter resides,
We'll toast to the secrets, the fun that abides.
For every lost shoe and forgotten old grin,
Brings a chuckle and warmth, let the dreaming begin!

Echoes in a Hidden Space

In a nook hidden well, whispers flit and glide,
Of lovers long lost and catfights that chide.
The echo of laughter bounces off walls,
As sock puppets hold court at their furry ball.

Underneath a old quilt, a ghost tries to sing,
About banana peels and the joys they bring.
He tripped on the laughter, fell flat on his face,
And now every giggle just lives in this space.

A dance of the brooms, they twirl and they sway,
They sweep up the stories of yesterday.
The dust on their bristles holds tales oh so grand,
Of feasts that were held in the downy bandstand.

So let's raise a laugh for the echoes we find,
For love's silly whispers, and winks left behind.
In this hidden space where the giggles arise,
Life's funny little secrets wear sparkly ties.

Memories Stored in Shadows

In the shadowy corners where lost time expires,
Lie teddy bears dreaming by old, crackling fires.
They recall all the games that were played out of sight,
And how cake frosting took a daring flight.

A pair of old sneakers with stories to tell,
Of running to catch love, and slipping as well.
The laces once tangled now curl in retreat,
From races to nowhere, oh what a feat!

The ceiling fan laughs at a paper plane's flight,
That flipped through the room in a blur of delight.
It soared past the curtains, kissed dust in a whirl,
Leaving shadows behind of a mischievous girl.

So here's to the memories tucked neatly away,
In the funny, forgotten, whimsical display.
For in every shadow, a giggle you'll find,
And love's lightest moments, forever entwined.

The Weight of Unexpressed Yearnings

In a corner, dust bunnies play,
Wrestling dreams that went astray.
A sock puppet sighs with regret,
Lost chances wrapped in a pink cassette.

Beneath the beams, old secrets dwell,
A whistling teapot with tales to tell.
Every sigh is a giggle in disguise,
While moths flutter by with puzzled eyes.

Unused stationery, letters unsent,
Ink stains of love, long ago spent.
The cat nabs a plan, and it's a riot,
Curling up on my hopes, oh what a diet!

Yet amidst the clutter, smiles keep peeking,
Old photographs, memories are leaking.
A tickled heart in a whimsical race,
Tripping over joy in this cluttered space.

Notes From a Time Past

A trumpet from yesteryear toots,
As a calendar wears old, dusty boots.
The echo of shoes that danced on air,
Now nudges the memories — do they care?

Faded postcards of places unknown,
Giggles from friends who've long since flown.
Each stamp a reminder of wild escapades,
When we thought time was just a charade.

In a box labeled 'What Was I Thinking?'
Half-baked ideas, all quickly shrinking.
A recipe for joy turned into a mess,
With laughter and love, we still do confess.

As the wind whispers secrets to trees,
I collect silly tales carried on the breeze.
With a wink and a nod, they sit there still,
Waiting for hearts to cherish and thrill.

Silenced Songs in the Rafters

Up high where the cobwebs dream,
Are tunes that once danced like a sunbeam.
A guitar with strings made of wishes,
Piled high with notes and forgotten dishes.

Silly serenades from a scruffy bear,
Cuddle with laughter that lingers in air.
A kazoo plays the blues with flair,
As dust motes whirl in a merry affair.

Old music sheets with scribbles and dots,
Whisper about love tied in knots.
As laughter spills from a lopsided chair,
I'm reminded that joy is best shared with flair.

The rafters hum tales of delight,
In a room where the wrongs seem just right.
With each playful note that's unstrung,
Heartfelt giggles continue to be sung.

Recollections in Umber Shadows

Shadows painted in cocoa brown,
Whimsy and wonder all wrapped up in a gown.
Old chairs become thrones of delight,
As memories jiggle in the pale moonlight.

The squeak of a floorboard, a joke in disguise,
Where laughter erupts and flies to the skies.
Papery tales of jubilant spree,
With winks from the past that beg to be free.

A treasure trove of silliness stacked,
In corners where quirks have softly packed.
Every trinket has a story to share,
Like tangled hair that lost its flair.

Amidst the shadows, a mirth-filled riot,
A heart on a rollercoaster, oh so quiet.
With every chuckle that echoes around,
We savor the joy in the beauty we found.

www.ingramcontent.com/pod-product-compliance
Lightning Source LLC
Chambersburg PA
CBHW060126230426
43661CB00003B/349